GREAT EXIT PROJECTS ON THE
WOMEN'S RIGHTS MOVEMENT

GREAT SOCIAL STUDIES EXIT PROJECTS™

HEAR OUR VOICES

GREAT EXIT PROJECTS ON THE
WOMEN'S RIGHTS MOVEMENT

Bethany Bryan

rosen publishing's
rosen central®

New York

Published in 2020 by The Rosen Publishing Group, Inc.
29 East 21st Street, New York, NY 10010

First Edition

Library of Congress Cataloging-in-Publication Data

Names: Bryan, Bethany, author.
Title: Great exit projects on the women's rights movement / Bethany Bryan.
Description: New York : Rosen Publishing, 2020 | Series: Great social studies exit projects |
Audience: Grades 5–8. | Includes bibliographical references and index.
Identifiers: LCCN 2018012923| ISBN 9781499440553 (library bound) | ISBN 9781499440546 (pbk.)
Subjects: LCSH: Women's rights—Juvenile literature. | Feminism—Juvenile literature.
Classification: LCC HQ1236 .B79 2019 | DDC 305.42—dc23
LC record available at https://lccn.loc.gov/2018012923

Manufactured in the United States of America

CONTENTS

INTRODUCTION

The phrase "A woman's place is in the home" can be traced back to the writings of Greek playwright Aeschylus in 467 BCE. In the play *Seven Against Thebes*, the character of Eteocles says, "It is for the man to take care of business outside the house; let no woman make decrees in those matters. Keep inside and do no harm!" Variations of this phrase have remained popular through the centuries.

During that time, women across many societies have done just that: handled the role of mother and nurturer, wife, and caretaker of the home. Many women accept this role because of being raised in an environment where this is encouraged because of religious beliefs and tradition, because it's the logical economic choice for a family, or because she simply prefers to and feels it's her calling. Other women have ambitions to work outside of the home—to be a doctor, a chemist, an astronaut, a dog walker, a mechanic, a writer, or something else entirely. But certain laws and traditions throughout history have prevented women from making that choice for themselves. They've been prevented from voting, owning property, having the right to marry whomever they choose, seek a divorce, get an education and a job, and to make their own reproductive choices. This is where the fight for women's rights comes in.

The women's rights movement in the United States began officially in the late 1840s, with a group of women who believed that women deserved the same rights as men. They believed that this change would be possible if they attained, for all women, the right to vote. Voting rights would allow women some say in government, ultimately giving them more power to make their

Mrs. Herbert Carpenter was one of the women who walked down Fifth Avenue in New York City during a march for women's rights held early in the twentieth century.

own choices. From there, the movement grew and has evolved over the years, as now issues have arisen and need to be addressed. The US Constitution was amended to allow women to vote in 1920. But the fight wasn't over by a long shot. Even with the ability to vote, new issues came to light. Women are still fighting for their rights today, not only in North America but all over the world. This ongoing fight is one in which women's rights activists of all genders and ages have an important role to play.

As students explore women's rights as part of the social studies curriculum, they are often called upon to create an exit project (also sometimes known as a culminating project) that shows how well they have learned the material and how they can apply it to their own lives. This project is focused on asking thought-provoking questions and answering them through research, contemplation, and creativity. This guide is not intended to provide a project for this purpose, but to give students the tools for creating one of their own.

CHAPTER ONE

THE CONVENTION AT SENECA FALLS

In the town of Waterloo, New York, on July 13, 1848, a group of women—Lucretia Mott, Elizabeth Cady Stanton, Martha Wright, and Mary Ann McClintock—got together for

This statue stands at Seneca Falls to commemorate the 1851 meeting of Susan B. Anthony (*left*) and her friend and collaborator Elizabeth Cady Stanton (*right*).

a tea party at the home of a friend named Jane Hunt. Tea was served, and as the guests sipped their drinks, the talk turned to politics. The women were unhappy at not being allowed to vote and not being allowed to own property, among other grievances. They felt that the Declaration of Independence, which had promised freedom to all Americans, was focused only on the rights of men and excluded women. As the women talked, they decided that they needed to take action, and they formed a plan. The women would schedule the first women's rights convention, to take place only six days later, at the Wesleyan Chapel in Seneca Falls, a town just a few miles away. They wrote and posted notices to help bring in more attendees—and their hard work paid off. Six days after the tea party that started it all, about three hundred attendees, both men and women, arrived at the chapel for the very first American women's rights convention.

On the first morning of the convention, Elizabeth Cady Stanton stood before the assembly and read a new Declaration of Independence, one that would help set the agenda for the event and for the future of women's rights. This document was called the Declaration of Sentiments, and it would mirror the structure of the Declaration of Independence, but outlining a number of rights that women had previously been denied.

QUESTION 1 WOMEN FELT EXCLUDED FROM THE DECLARATION OF INDEPENDENCE. IN WHAT WAYS DID THE DECLARATION OF SENTIMENTS COMPENSATE FOR THAT OMISSION?

The main points of the Declaration of Sentiments were that these women wanted the right to vote, to own property, and to find gainful employment. They wanted equal rights under the law, to get a quality education, to be granted a fair divorce, and for men to be held to the same moral standards as women. The United States had been founded on the idea of liberty, and yet women were still facing limitations under the law.

Not everyone agreed with the points laid out by the Declaration of Sentiments, however. Even Lucretia Mott was opposed to asking for equal voting rights because she felt it detracted from some of the other important points, and she wasn't alone in this opinion. There was also a firm divide from the beginning of the movement over how much overlap there should be with the abolitionist movement. At the time, slavery was still legal. Should these women fight only for their own rights or should their work include a fight for the civil rights and freedom of all men and women in the United States? Where should they draw the line?

PROJECT 1
A CLOSER LOOK AT THE DECLARATION OF SENTIMENTS

Some people believed that the Declaration of Sentiments did not go far enough. Others believed that it went too far. Using the Declaration of Sentiments and the Declaration of Independence as primary sources, analyze their strengths and weaknesses.

- Read through the Declaration of Independence carefully. You can find it at https://www.archives.gov /founding-docs/declaration-transcript.
- Read through the Declaration of Sentiments carefully, which can be found at http://ecssba.rutgers.edu/docs /seneca.html.

A lot of information about the early women's rights movement and its key players can be found online. A library is also a good place to start!

- Do you feel that these documents, in combination, compensate for the rights of all Americans? If not, consider what you would add or change to make the documents apply to everyone. Write your changes down or keep track of them in a spreadsheet.
- Next, write your own Declaration of Sentiments, or a declaration with the name of your choosing, based on current events and the experiences of modern Americans. You will want to consider how different groups of people

are treated under US law and what groups of people may not have needed legal protections.

- Read back through your declaration. How does it compare with the originals? Think about how these documents contributed to US society and government and how you would hope your document would contribute to US society and government as well.
- Compile your findings into a PowerPoint presentation (or use a free presentation software like Google Deck) and share your Declaration of Sentiments with your classmates. Take questions and suggestions. In what ways should you amend the document now that you've received feedback from your peers?

ELIZABETH CADY STANTON

Elizabeth Cady was born in Johnstown, New York, on November 12, 1815, to parents who supported her ambition. After graduation, she began to study the law at her father's law office, by reading and listening in to the conversations going on around her. Elizabeth quickly grew to support the antislavery movement in the United States and soon met and married a fellow abolitionist, Henry Stanton. For the couple's honeymoon, they attended the World's Antislavery Convention in London, where Elizabeth met Lucretia Mott. The two would help organize the Seneca Falls Convention, where Elizabeth Cady Stanton presented the Declaration of Sentiments to the assembly.

A lifelong advocate of human rights, she did not live to see women receive the right to vote, but Stanton is regarded as one of the most important figures of the women's rights movement.

QUESTION 2 HOW DID THE WOMEN OF THE WOMEN'S RIGHTS MOVEMENT COME TOGETHER FOR THE SAME CAUSE?

The women's rights movement in the United States began because a group of women got together to share their personal struggles and their hopes for the future. They shared similar experiences and wanted similar things. A convention brings a group of people with shared interests together. These can be political, business-related, or for entertainment. The Seneca Falls Convention helped to generate interest in the cause, bring women and men together to unite under that cause, and ignite the flame of activism so that the cause could continue to move forward, even after the convention was long over.

PROJECT 2
PLANNING A WOMEN'S RIGHTS CONVENTION

In this project, you can plan and present your own convention for women's rights—which continues to be a relevant issue to organize around.

- In a group of three to five fellow classmates, begin to brainstorm your own plans for a mock women's rights convention. What issues would you want to see addressed by the convention? Are there any differing ideas about what needs to be addressed and how? Work out these differences in opinion and create a unified strategy.
- Assign each member of the group a task. What strengths does each member bring to the table? How might

14

members' different personal interests or perspectives inform your convention?

- Consider how you would use modern technology to spread the word about your convention. Would you bring in famous speakers to help generate interest in the event? Whom would you hire?
- Plan a program for the event. Where would it be held? What events would you schedule? How would you hold the interest of attendees?
- Present your plan for the convention to your classmates.

QUESTION 3 IN WHAT WAYS WERE THE ABOLITION MOVEMENT AND WOMEN'S RIGHTS MOVEMENT LINKED?

Women weren't the only attendees of the Seneca Falls Convention. Many men were in attendance as well, including Frederick Douglass, who was a former slave and a longtime activist in the abolition movement. Douglass was one of the thirty-two men who signed the Declaration of Sentiments and the only African American in attendance. He believed in universal suffrage, which would give voting rights to all men and all women.

Soon after the Seneca Falls Convention came to an end, Frederick Douglass wrote of his experience in his antislavery newspaper, *The North Star*:

In respect to political rights, we hold woman to be justly entitled to all we claim for man. We go farther, and express our conviction that all political rights which it is expedient for man to exercise, it is equally so for women. All that distinguishes man as an intelligent and accountable being, is equally true of woman; and if that government is only just which governs by the free consent of the governed, there can be no reason in the world for denying to woman the exercise of the elective franchise, or a hand in making and administering the laws of the land. Our doctrine is, that "Right is of no sex."

Many abolitionists, like Douglass, also believed in the necessity of equal rights for women. In fact, many activists and their families, including the Stantons and the Motts, began their activism as abolitionists. In this way, the women's rights movement developed from abolition, and both involved fights for social justice for all people, regardless of race or gender.

PROJECT 3
FREDERICK DOUGLASS FIGHTS FOR RIGHTS FOR ALL

Frederick Douglass was a staunch fighter for equal rights for all American citizens. In this project, explore his biography and his passion for social justice through writing a short one-act play.

- Research the life and activism of Frederick Douglass either online or in your school or public library.
  - o How did Douglass's early life lead to activism as an adult?
  - o What actions early in his life as an activist made him well known?
  - o Describe the challenges that Frederick Douglass faced during his life and how they changed.

Frederick Douglass was a powerful voice in the abolitionist movement, but he also advocated for equal rights for women and attended the convention at Seneca Falls.

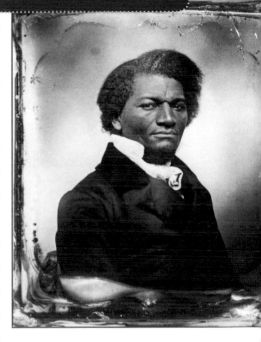

- o How did his advocacy of women's rights strengthen both the abolitionist movement and the women's rights movement?
- o How was Douglass similar to other activists of his time period? How was he different?

- Create a one-act play about Frederick Douglass deciding to attend the Seneca Falls Convention. You may include scenes in which he speaks with leading abolitionists and women's rights activists of the time and scenes illustrating how his actions may have been both admired and criticized by fellow activists.
- Perform your work for the class.

CHAPTER TWO

THE LEADERS OF THE MOVEMENT

Out of all of the relationships forged by the women's rights movement, the most important of these was the one between Elizabeth Cady Stanton and Susan B. Anthony.

Susan B. Anthony was born in Adams, Massachusetts, in 1820, in a Quaker home where antislavery advocacy and temperance were both important. The family moved to Rochester, New York, in 1845, and Anthony's brothers, Daniel and Merritt, left soon after the move to work for the abolitionist cause in Kansas, where tensions were high over the issue. Anthony became a teacher, but her activism continued.

In this famous photo, Elizabeth Cady Stanton and Susan B. Anthony, the founders of the National Woman Suffrage Association, pose together in 1881.

In 1951, Susan B. Anthony traveled to Seneca Falls to attend an abolitionist convention. It was there that she met Elizabeth Cady Stanton. Said Stanton of their meeting, "There she stood with her good, earnest face and genial smile, dressed In gray delaine, hat and all the same color, relieved with pale blue ribbons, the perfection of neatness and sobriety. I liked her thoroughly, and why I did not at once invite her home with me to dinner, I do not know."

QUESTION 4 WHAT PRINCIPLES DID SUSAN B. ANTHONY AND ELIZABETH CADY STANTON FEEL STRONGLY ABOUT? HOW DID THEY, TOGETHER, REPRESENT THE WOMEN'S RIGHTS MOVEMENT?

Susan B. Anthony and Elizabeth Cady Stanton became fast friends. Together they founded the *Revolution*, a women's newspaper, and the National Woman Suffrage Association. Stanton handled much of the writing and public-facing commentary, while Anthony managed the business side of their work, strategizing and organizing the movement.

Anna Howard Shaw, an activist who took up the women's suffrage cause at the urging of Susan B. Anthony once wrote of the relationship between Anthony and Stanton:

> She [Miss Anthony] often said that Mrs. Stanton was the brains of the new association, while she herself was merely its hands and feet; but in truth the two women worked marvelously together, for Mrs. Stanton was a master of words and could write and speak to perfection of the things Susan B. Anthony saw and felt but could not herself express.

PROJECT 4
THE WRITINGS OF SUSAN B. ANTHONY AND ELIZABETH CADY STANTON

Susan B. Anthony and Elizabeth Cady Stanton both kept diaries, as did many during this time period, as a method of record keeping. They also wrote letters to other members of the cause and each other, as Elizabeth Cady Stanton had children and often found it difficult to travel.

One of the best ways to learn about the women's rights movement is to explore primary sources such as letters and essays. You might even want to make photocopies.

- Explore the collected writings of Susan B. Anthony and Elizabeth Cady Stanton using the Elizabeth Cady Stanton & Susan B. Anthony Papers Project through Rutgers University's website at http://ecssba.rutgers.edu/index.html.
- Create a list of the things that concern each woman the most.
  o What issues come up again and again?
  o Who are their chief allies?
  o Who seems to be working against them?
  o What solutions do they come up with to aid in the cause?
- Write five diary entries or letters each for both Elizabeth Cady Stanton and Susan B. Anthony using a blogging site like LiveJournal or Wordpress, outlining these principles and capturing the strengths and voice of each woman.

WHO ARE THE QUAKERS?

Quakerism was founded by an Englishman named George Fox during the 1600s, when many in England were starting their own churches. Officially known as the Religious Society of Friends, the Quakers believe that spirituality comes from within, not from a church. By the mid-1650s, Quaker missionaries were making their way to the New World. In the colonies, many Quakers found the religious freedom they had been seeking and positions of power within the Colonial government—under the rule of the British monarchy, of course.

(continued on the next page)

(continued from the previous page)

Quakers were pacifists, meaning that they rejected war and violence. Therefore, they were quick to pick up the cause of protecting the rights of Native Americans and African enslaved people. That Susan B. Anthony and Lucretia Mott were both Quakers was no coincidence! Both believed strongly in human rights because of their religious beliefs.

Lucretia Mott was also considered one of the leading voices of the women's rights movement during this era. Born a Quaker, like Susan B. Anthony, Mott grew up in the Hudson Valley in

New York and became a teacher at the Quaker boarding school she had attended as a child. In 1811, she married fellow instructor James Mott, and the two had six children together. But after her eldest son died, Lucretia Mott devoted herself to her religious beliefs and soon became a Quaker minister.

After joining the women's rights movement, Mott often played the role of peacemaker. She was one of the older members of the movement and was often looked to for her skills in diplomacy as differences of

Lucretia Mott, like many Quakers, was a staunch opponent of slavery. When she was excluded from an abolitionist meeting in 1833, she founded the Female Anti-Slavery Society.

opinion arose. During her later years, as she struggled with that role and several challenging physical ailments, she focused her efforts on simply helping those who needed her voice.

Lucy Stone was also one of the important leaders of the movement, although her name is not as well known today. Stone was a brilliant lecturer during a time when a popular form of entertainment was attending lectures and engaging in politics. After completing her education, she was hired to work for the American Anti-Slavery Society, for which she wrote and delivered many speeches. Stone quickly became one of the most famous women in the United States, but fame came with the price of notoriety and she was sometimes heckled and even endured physical attacks. Two years after the Seneca Falls Convention, she organized a similar convention in Worcester, Massachusetts, and because of her fame, her speech was printed internationally, taking the movement global.

QUESTION 5 COMPARE THE ACTIVISM OF SUSAN B. ANTHONY, ELIZABETH CADY STANTON, LUCRETIA MOTT, LUCY STONE, AND OTHER PROMINENT MEMBERS OF THE MOVEMENT WITH MODERN ACTIVISM FOR WOMEN'S RIGHTS. HOW DO THEIR ACTIONS COMPARE TO THOSE OF MODERN WOMEN'S RIGHTS ACTIVISTS?

PROJECT 5
ACTIVISM TODAY AND YESTERDAY

Every movement needs a leader, and the women's rights movement in the United States had many, including Susan B.

Anthony, Elizabeth Cady Stanton, Lucretia Mott, Lucy Stone, and others. There were issues that they agreed upon and issues that caused rifts.

- Research two of these prominent leaders of the women's rights movement, focusing on their backgrounds and history.
- Investigate a similar partnership or group that exists in America today.
- Consider how these women approached activism. What were the downsides of protest during the mid- to late nineteenth century?
- How do modern leaders approach this type of activism? What are the downsides of protest today? What are the positives?
- Write an imagined conversation between two of these modern leaders as they plan a protest today. How would they communicate? Who would they recommend inviting?
- Partner up with a classmate and deliver this conversation to your class.

One of the fiercest dividing points that affected the women's rights movement was how much thought and care should be given to the link between women's rights and human rights. Was the fight limited to winning voting rights for women, or was the larger goal to acquire voting rights for all?

In 1870, the Fifteenth Amendment was passed and adopted into the Constitution. This outraged many women's rights activists because it granted voting rights only to all men, when women of all races were still unable to vote, despite decades of work. Many in the movement began to advocate exclusively for the rights of white women, often ignoring the voices of people of color. Said activist Anna Howard Shaw, "You have put the ballot in the hands of your black men, thus making them political superiors of white women. Never before in the history of the world have men made former slaves the political masters of their former mistresses!" This belief system caused a rift in the movement that wouldn't be repaired for decades.

The National Woman Suffrage Association (NWSA), founded by Susan B. Anthony and Elizabeth Cady Stanton, refused to support the Fifteenth Amendment unless it included voting rights for women. Women's rights activists who supported the Fifteenth Amendment as it was, including Lucy Stone, formed the American Woman Suffrage Association (AWSA). It is important to note here that although black men received the right to vote, they were often prevented from doing so by discriminatory practices and threats of violence.

QUESTION 6 WHAT ROLE DID AFRICAN AMERICAN WOMEN PLAY IN THE WOMEN'S RIGHTS MOVEMENT DURING THIS ERA?

One popular misconception about women's suffrage that still exists today is that it was fought and won by white women only, but African American women played a significant, pivotal role. One of the most outspoken of these women's rights activists was Sojourner Truth.

Born with the name Isabella Baumfree, Truth lived as a slave in the northern states. She was bought and sold many times as a child and suffered horrible abuse at the hands of her masters. She served a family in New Paltz, New York, until 1827, when she escaped slavery by moving to the home of a Quaker family and adopting their last name. A year later, slaves were freed in the state of New York, and she could live as a free woman. She soon moved to New York, where she began to share her beliefs with the public by preaching her sermons on the streets. Truth was 6 feet (2 meters) tall and had a powerful speaking voice. People began to take notice, and her truth-telling speeches grew in popularity. Soon, she was traveling all over the United States to give lectures on abolition, women's rights, and temperance. Isabella changed her name to Sojourner Truth in 1843.

PROJECT 6
A CLOSER LOOK AT SOJOURNER TRUTH'S "AIN'T I A WOMAN?"

In 1851, Sojourner Truth traveled to Akron, Ohio, for a speaking engagement. There, she gave her most famous speech. Although she never learned to read and write, she was masterful at composing powerful, influential words.

- Read through Sojourner Truth's "Ain't I a Woman?" speech at https://www.nps.gov/articles/sojourner-truth.htm.
- What about this work resonates with you?
- How did Sojourner Truth's feelings on womanhood differ from those of her white contemporaries?
- How did African American women like Sojourner Truth face a "double bind" in terms of being repressed due to both their gender and their race?
- Read "Women's Suffrage Leaders Left Out Black Women" by Evette Dionne in *Teen Vogue* online. Do you think the

Sojourner Truth was known for her powerful speaking voice. Her "Ain't I a Woman?" speech is one of the most important of the women's rights movement.

first-wave women's rights movement did enough for African American women, such as Sojourner Truth? Why or why not?

- Create a presentation using PowerPoint or a similar tool, collecting the information you have found. Make sure to address how African American women were excluded in many ways from the women's rights movement and whether or not you feel that exclusion continues in some way today.

CHAPTER THREE

THE NINETEENTH AMENDMENT

By 1890, the animosity of the previous two decades had finally cooled, and the two main women's rights organizations were able to merge again, forming the National American Woman Suffrage Association (NAWSA). Elizabeth Cady Stanton, then around seventy-five years of age, stepped up into the role of the first president of the organization and served for two years.

The agenda of women's suffrage had evolved in the forty-two years since Seneca Falls. The issue of prohibition—the outlaw of alcohol—had moved closer to the forefront. The group was focusing on using amendments at the state level to push for a federal amendment. They had also changed their approach to equality. No longer were they "created equal to men." They now embraced being different from men. Theoretically, they thought, a vote cast by a woman would create a more moral, maternal government than one wherein men made all the rules.

American women were also changing. They were joining the workforce in record numbers, making up 17.2 percent by 1890, according to the National Bureau of Economic Research, an almost 3 percent increase over twenty years. They were

Suffragist Anna Howard Shaw can be seen standing at center as she delivers a speech to a gathering of the National American Woman Suffrage Association (NAWSA).

becoming more progressive, and this wasn't a coincidence. For over forty years, Elizabeth Cady Stanton, Susan B. Anthony, and the other members of the women's rights movement had traveled across the country for speaking engagements. Their ideas were spreading and taking hold.

QUESTION 7 HOW DID THE IDEAS AND PRINCIPLES OF THE WOMEN'S RIGHTS MOVEMENT SPREAD ACROSS THE UNITED STATES?

In 1861, women in Kansas were granted the right to vote in school board elections. In 1867, a proposal to amend the Kansas Constitution allowing women the right to vote appeared on the ballot. The amendment was voted down, but just a few years later, the Wyoming Territory did pass a law allowing women the right to vote. Wyoming was followed by other western states, including Colorado and Utah.

PROJECT 7

THE MOVEMENT OF A MOVEMENT

In this project, create a timeline and map of the spread of women's suffrage in the United States.

- Create a timeline of the women's rights movement similar to the one shown here: https://www.scholastic.com /teachers/articles/teaching-content/important-dates -us-womens-history. Take note of the locations of these events.
- Using a GPS app or Google Maps, find and note the latitude and longitude of these locations in a spreadsheet or other means of recording data.
- Find a printable map of the continental United States online or use a laminated wall map that can be reused.
- Using the coordinates of landmark events in the history of women's rights, map out how the movement spread from

1948 until the passage of the Nineteenth Amendment in 1920.

- Think about why women's suffrage spread the way it did. Why might women's suffrage have begun largely in the western part of the United States?
- Present your map to your class, describing the geography of progress.

QUESTION 8 WHAT MOTIVATED THE ACTIONS OF THE ANTISUFFRAGE MOVEMENT? WHAT REASONS DID THEY HAVE TO OPPOSE SUFFRAGE FOR WOMEN?

The women's rights movement had always faced adversity, but as it started to grow and make inroads around the country, opposition grew right along with it. But antisuffragists didn't really organize until the early 1900s, with the founding of the National Association Opposed to Woman Suffrage (NAOWS) in 1911. Although many men had voiced a steady opposition, the antisuffragists were actually led by women.

The president of NAOWS was Josephine Jewell Dodge, the daughter of Marshall Jewell, who had served as the US minister to Russia in the 1870s, as well as acting as postmaster general. In 1875, Josephine married Arthur Dodge, a man who came from a prominent New York family. For her part in the movement, Josephine worked toward establishing some child care programs for poverty-stricken women who had to join the workforce. She believed that suffrage would only increase this necessity, rather than allowing women to maintain their traditional roles as caregivers to their children.

PROJECT 8
A CLOSER LOOK AT THE ANTISUFFRAGIST AGENDA

Research the arguments of the antisuffragists and how suffragettes responded to these criticisms.

- The National Association Opposed to Woman Suffrage outlined their reasons for opposing allowing women to have the right to vote. They can be seen here: https://www.loc.gov/resource/rbpe.1300130c. You can also read antisuffrage essays through Project Gutenberg: https://www.gutenberg.orgfiles/35689/35689-h/35689-h.htm.

Project Gutenberg is an online collection of electronic books, many of which are no longer in print. It's a good place to begin your research.

- Think about the following question: What are the antisuffragists' three most powerful arguments against women's suffrage?
- Research the writings of a suffragist who was a contemporary of the antisuffragist movement, such as Carrie Chapman Catt. Her writings are collected here: https://asteria.fivecolleges.edu/findaids/sophiasmith/mnsss144.html.
- How would a suffragist like Carrie Chapman Catt counter the three main arguments made by the antisuffragists?
- What arguments would you make against the antisuffragist agenda?
- Create a PowerPoint presentation that details the main arguments of the antisuffragist agenda, how these arguments were countered during the time period they were made, and how you would counter them today.
- Share your presentation with your class, allowing them to discuss the different viewpoints. What has changed in the century since the antisuffrage movement? What remains the same? Are there still arguments from the antisuffrage movement that are used today?

QUESTION 9 HOW DID THE PASSAGE OF THE NINETEENTH AMENDMENT CHANGE SOCIETY?

As the twentieth century began, the face of the women's movement began to change. New women's suffrage activists were picking up the cause as the older generation began to die. Lucretia Mott had died in 1880, followed by Lucy Stone in 1893. Elizabeth Cady Stanton died in 1902, followed by

Susan B. Anthony in 1906. But many of their daughters—including Stanton's daughter Harriot Stanton Blatch—and those who were influenced by their work, including Carrie Chapman Catt, were happy to carry the torch of the new generation.

Change was happening. Utah, Idaho, and Colorado had joined Wyoming in allowing women the right to vote by the turn of the century. Kansas, Arizona, Alaska, Illinois, and Oregon soon followed. But the women's rights movement was about to split in two once again. In 1913, the National Woman's Party (NWP) was founded by Alice Paul and Lucy Burns. The goal of their organization was to revive the long-dead issue of passing a Constitutional amendment on women's suffrage. With progress at the state level, a Constitutional amendment seemed more possible than it had ever been. This was a departure from the current agenda of the National American Woman Suffrage Association (NAWSA), then led by Carrie Chapman Catt. Their goal was to pinpoint areas in the United States where suffrage was facing a tougher resistance and work to campaign in those regions. They called this the Winning Plan. The NAWSA continued a quiet, traditional campaign as they had always done, but the National Woman's Party was far more radical and militant.

President Woodrow Wilson took office in 1913. He had run a campaign opposed to women's suffrage, but he had three daughters who had grown up smart and independent. Many in the women's rights movement, including Alice Paul, saw this as an opportunity to try and change his mind. The National Woman's Party began to picket the White House regularly, beginning in 1917, amid the carnage of World War I, which had slowed progress within the women's movement. They not only protested for suffrage but also about the war. At first, their protests were peaceful. President Wilson even invited them in for coffee. About six months into their campaign, things changed. In June 1917, six of the protestors were arrested, followed by more arrests in the following weeks. Wilson found their behavior to be unladylike and offensive. They were charged with "obstructing traffic" and sentenced to sixty days in the workhouse—a prisonlike house or farm where residents worked to repay debts. (These fell out of favor after the passage of the Social Security Act in 1935.) But the protests continued.

Finally, Carrie Chapman Catt stepped in, seeing an opportunity. She and the other members of the NAWSA had

In 1917, NAWSA leaders met with Woodrow Wilson. Anna Howard Shaw stands in the front row, second from the left, and Carrie Chapman Catt is second from right.

always eschewed protest tactics like the ones the members of the National Woman's Party had engaged in. Congress was preparing to vote again on a women's suffrage amendment. Catt made a plea to the president, showing support for the war effort while speaking out on behalf of the Constitutional amendment. This was an important turning point in the history of the women's rights movement and the fight for suffrage. Carrie Chapman Catt convinced President Wilson to change his mind. In an address to the Senate, Wilson expressed his support for a Constitutional amendment allowing women the right to vote. Although it would not pass officially until 1920, the tide had turned. The Nineteenth Amendment was ratified on August 18, 1920. American women, almost 145 years after the founding of the nation, had the right to vote.

THE LAST SURVIVOR

Of all of the sixty-eight women who signed the Declaration of Sentiments at the Seneca Falls Convention in 1848, only one lived to see the passage of the Nineteenth Amendment. Charlotte Woodward was only eighteen or nineteen years old when she heard about the convention and decided to attend. "I wanted to work, but I wanted to choose my task and I wanted to collect my wages," she said later of what the convention meant to her at the time. She traveled about 40 miles (64 kilometers) to attend, the greatest recorded distance traveled by any of the attendees.

Seventy-two years later, on Election Day in 1920, Woodward was ill and didn't get the chance to cast a vote. "I'm too old." she said. "I'm afraid I'll never vote." She passed away a year later at the age of ninety-two.

PROJECT 9
THE SUFFRAGE MOVEMENT DRAWS TO A CLOSE

Research one American suffragist, analyze the work she did, and write a letter to her explaining how her actions changed life for women today.

- Research the American suffragists listed so far in this volume.
- Choose one whose values seem to align most closely with your own or whose work you find to be the most influential.
- Write out a list of the issues this suffragist felt most strongly about.
- Compose a letter to this suffragist, telling her about the impact she has made in your life and in the United States today.
- Create a supporting hashtag and, with your parents' permission, share your letter via Twitter or Facebook. Collect any thoughtful, engaging responses you receive and present them to your class, along with the original letter. What did you learn, if anything, from those with whom you shared your letter?

CHAPTER FOUR

THE SECOND WAVE

Women finally had the right to vote in the United States. As a result, Carrie Chapman Catt founded the League of Women Voters (LWV) in 1920. This group would go on to help women voters carry out their responsibility and enact change for themselves. It continues to do so today. But suffrage was never the end goal for women's rights. The fight moved onward to new issues facing American women.

More and more women were joining the workforce, especially in the wake of World War I. They began to notice that as women it was harder to get a job and make a living than it was for a man because of archaic hiring practices and disparity in pay.

Additionally, women were finally gaining the ability to

Margaret Sanger remains a controversial figure, but her efforts helped many women gain access to birth control in the early to mid-twentieth century.

make their own choices when it came to family planning. In 1916, a former nurse and social reformer named Margaret Sanger opened the first birth control clinic in Brooklyn, New York, and immediately faced backlash from the public. The United States was going through an era during which "morality" was at the forefront, especially for policy makers. For example, the late 1800s and early 1900s saw a rise in recreational drug use around the United States, resulting in calls for bans and regulation. In 1919, the Eighteenth Amendment was ratified, banning the manufacture and distribution of alcohol. The Comstock Act had banned distribution of birth control or any related materials in 1873. So Margaret Sanger was facing a hostile public when it came to issues surrounding birth control distribution. The public atmosphere for the first birth control clinic was a hostile one, but Sanger knew that the work she was doing was important, so she endured repeated arrests and harassment.

QUESTION 10 HOW DOES GIVING WOMEN CONTROL OVER FAMILY PLANNING AND CONTRACEPTION AID IN THE LARGER FIGHT FOR ECONOMIC JUSTICE FOR WOMEN?

Birth control had long existed in the United States, with the introduction of condoms and diaphragms around 1838, but Margaret Sanger's birth control clinic signaled to many that immorality was on the rise. Finally, in 1938, through Sanger's efforts, a federal judge ruled to lift the ban on birth control devices in the United States, overturning part of the Comstock Act. But the development of birth control didn't stop there. Condoms, diaphragms, and cervical caps—which had been introduced to the American public in the 1920s—were often ineffective and hard to get. Margaret Sanger was looking for something more foolproof, smaller, and easier to use—ideally a pill.

Around 1950, she approached a man named Gregory Goodwin Pincus to help make this plan a reality. Pincus was a scientist specializing in the reproductive sciences, and he was game for taking on this controversial task, which many others had turned down in the conservative 1950s. Pincus teamed up with Dr. M. C. Chang of the Worcester Foundation for Experimental Biology and a gynecologist named John Rock. By 1960, they had developed a pill that used synthesized hormones in order to control ovulation. Enovid was soon approved by the Food and Drug Administration. By 1962, 1.2 million American women were on the pill. By 1965, that number was 6.5 million.

Allowing women greater control over their bodies instituted some important economic changes as well. As women were able to take part in choosing how large they wanted their family to be, they had more control over their professional lives as well. Choosing to have fewer children often meant an increased chance to work outside the home. According to Planned Parenthood, by 1970, just five years after the birth control pill became legal, there was a 20 percent increase in women graduating from college. Many of these women began to enter the workforce.

PROJECT 10
THE ECONOMICS OF THE PILL

After the Pill was legalized in 1965, the amount of women pursuing degrees and entering the workforce increased dramatically. In this project, research the connection between economic opportunities for women and birth control.

Talking to other women and girls can help you to gain a new perspective on the women's rights movement. You'll never know what you'll learn!

- Using the Department of Labor Women's Bureau website (https://www.dol.gov/wb/stats/stats_data.htm), research the number of women in the labor force prior to 1965 and following 1965, as well as their earnings during these time periods.
- Make note of the statistics for women in the labor force in 1955, 1965, 1975, 1985, 1995, 2005, and 2015. What do you notice in terms of a trend? Keep track of your data in a spreadsheet.

- Ask yourself the following questions: How did the birth control pill contribute to this change in women's participation in the labor force? What else may have contributed to this? How has women's participation in the labor force changed recently? What improvements can still be made?
- Using PowerPoint, Google Deck, or another online tool, create a presentation with the data you've found. Make sure you include your interpretation of this data and your suggestions for future growth for women's participation in the labor force.

THE EQUAL PAY ACT OF 1963

In the early nineteenth century, women made up 25 percent of the American workforce, but despite doing the same or similar jobs as their male counterparts, many were paid significantly less. By 1960, the average white woman was still making two-thirds of what white men were making for doing the same job—black and Hispanic women were making even less. The Equal Pay Act was passed by Congress and signed into law by John F. Kennedy in 1963, and while many argue that it fixed pay equality, the bill was full of loopholes that allowed the issues to continue.

Many businesses continued to pay men a higher wage on the basis of seniority or productivity or for other reasons. Therefore, it was difficult for women to prove that they were being paid less than men because of their gender. Pay disparity between genders continues today.

QUESTION 11 WHAT WERE THE CHIEF PRINCIPLES OF THE SECOND WAVE OF THE WOMEN'S RIGHTS MOVEMENT?

The 1960s and the birth control pill ushered in a new women's movement that pushed back against the moral leanings of the early half of the twentieth century. This movement is called second-wave feminism. In 1963, the author and activist Betty Friedan published her philosophical text *The Feminine Mystique*, which addressed some of the newer issues women were facing, like finding a good career and emotional fulfillment. Friedan also fought for the right of women to have access to safe abortion

After the passage of the Nineteenth Amendment, the women's rights movement changed with the times. At this 1977 march, Betty Friedan can be seen at right in a red coat.

services. The Comstock Act of 1873 had banned the use of abortion drugs, and women were putting their lives at risk, seeking unsafe abortion services from untrained, unlicensed abortionists or attempting to take care of the issue at home. Betty Friedan also wanted to engage more women in politics and the policies that affected their lives. That is why she cofounded the National Organization for Women (NOW) and the National Women's Political Caucus (NWPC).

Another important figure in women's rights during this time was Gloria Steinem. During the 1960s, Steinem made a name for herself as a writer. She went on to found *Ms.* magazine, which covered women-focused topics like domestic violence, and was also involved with forming the National Women's Political Caucus. For second-wave activists like Steinem and Friedan, the fight for women's rights was largely economic. They believed strongly that women should not be constrained by the role of caretaker and that they should have control over their family planning so that they could enter the workforce and have some economic freedom.

At every stage of the women's rights movement, however, there have been women on the other side of the spectrum, standing in opposition to their progress. For Betty Friedan, Gloria Steinem, and the other important figures of the second wave, this opponent was Phyllis Schlafly.

Phyllis Schlafly, a self-proclaimed antifeminist, was an advocate for "traditional" roles for women. She spoke out against issues like abortion and equal pay because she believed that equal rights for women would lead to America's downfall. The Equal Rights Amendment (ERA) was the result of years of effort on the part of women's rights activists and a cornerstone of the second-wave women's movement. The ERA was designed to grant equal legal rights to all American citizens, regardless of sex, and particularly in terms of divorce, property, employment, and other economic concerns. It was passed by Congress in 1972, but because it was an amendment to the Constitution, it would need to be ratified by thirty-eight of the fifty states. Phyllis Schlafly fought fiercely against the amendment. In 1982, with only thirty-five states having ratified the amendment, it was shelved.

PROJECT 11
THE FIGHT FOR EQUAL RIGHTS

- Read about the ERA at https://www .equalrightsamendment.org. What is the purpose of the amendment? What does it state?
- Read Phyllis Schlafly's "'Equal Rights' for Women: Wrong Then, and Wrong Now," published in the *Los Angeles Times* on April 8, 2007.
- Write a list of Phyllis Schlafly's beliefs. What does she stand for? What is she opposed to?
- Why is Schlafly concerned about closing the "wage gap" for women? What economic rights for women does she say the passage of the ERA threatened?
- Write a two-page essay responding to Phyllis Schlafly. Do you agree or disagree with her? Do you think the ERA should be passed? What do you think about Schlafly's ideas of what women's "traditional" roles should be in society?
- Present your essay to your class.

CHAPTER FIVE

MODERN WOMEN'S RIGHTS

Much has changed since that fateful day in Seneca Falls, New York, in 1848. In the United States, women achieved the right to vote. They entered the workforce—according to the Brookings Institute, the percentage of women over sixteen

Women are still fighting for equal rights today. This march took place on January 21, 2018, in Athens, Greece, as women demanded workplace equality and other rights.

who worked or actively looked for work between 1962 and 2000 rose from 37 percent to 61 percent. They took control of their reproductive rights, making decisions for themselves and their families. In generation after generation, women have shown that they are tireless in their efforts to achieve and maintain equality.

QUESTION 12 HOW HAS THE FIGHT FOR WOMEN'S RIGHTS PROGRESSED SINCE THE SENECA FALLS CONVENTION IN 1948? HOW DOES THE FIGHT FOR WOMEN'S RIGHTS TODAY COMPARE?

Today, women and their allies are keeping up the fight for equality. And although many of the issues have changed, many have remained consistently at the forefront of politics for women. And many women are simply fighting to be included in the conversation.

One of the most important fights in women's rights today is against sexual violence. The #MeToo movement was founded by a woman named Tarana Burke in 2007. Since 1998, around 17,700,000 women reported being the victim of a sexual assault. The #MeToo movement works to empower women—particularly women of color from low-income communities—by letting them know that they aren't alone. In 2017, the movement gained momentum when actress Alyssa Milano encouraged women to use the #MeToo hashtag to share their own experiences with sexual violence and harassment. The movement went global, and soon people of all genders, ages, and cultural backgrounds stepped forward to share their experiences.

Women are also still fighting for equality in the workplace and in education. Hiring practices continue to favor white men, especially in the fields of science, math, engineering, and technology. The STEM (Science Technology Engineering Math) Initiative works to encourage students, particularly girls, people of color, and those from low-income backgrounds to take an interest in these fields and fill the growing number of jobs in these areas.

One of the main arguments that has persisted in the women's movement since Seneca Falls is inclusivity. Today, transgender and gender nonconforming individuals want a place in the women's rights movement because they are also affected by sexual violence and bias in the workplace and education, often to a greater extent than cisgender women are. Women of color—particularly African American women, who have historically always played a role in the women's rights movement in the United States—continue to push for the larger conversation on race-based discrimination against women to be included in the movement.

PROJECT 12
WOMEN'S RIGHTS ACROSS THE GENERATIONS

- Schedule interviews with members of your family who represent four generations of women. If family members aren't available, you can speak to any women who lived during the 1930s through 1950s, 1960s through 1980s, 1990s up to 2010, and interview a peer or log your own opinions.
- Create a Venn diagram of shared issues that span generations and issues that are generation specific.
- Assessing your chart, what issues did women face in the mid-twentieth century that they are still confronting today?

o What issues no longer seem to be at the forefront?

o Why are they no longer relevant?

o What issues, if any, are unique to the current generation?

• Present your chart and your findings to your class.

THE FIGHT AGAINST VIOLENCE

One of the fears that women face on a daily basis is violence. According to the global women's rights organization Womankind Worldwide, one in three women in the world will experience an act of violence within her lifetime. One in ten will experience sexual violence. Additionally, on average, 38 percent of women who are murdered were killed by an intimate partner—a husband or a boyfriend.

UN Women is fighting back by working to educate girls between the ages of five and twenty-five about where violence begins, how to prevent it and educate those around them on violence prevention, and where to find support within their communities. It also works to educate men and boys on ways to prevent gender-based violence.

QUESTION 13 HOW DO WOMEN'S RIGHTS IN THE UNITED STATES TODAY COMPARE TO WOMEN'S RIGHTS AROUND THE GLOBE? IN WHAT WAYS ARE THEIR STRUGGLES UNIVERSAL, AND IN WHAT WAYS ARE THEY DIFFERENT BECAUSE OF GEOGRAPHY, CULTURE, AND POLITICS?

The women's rights movement is also not limited to the United States. Women all over the world are fighting for equality

After the election of US president Donald Trump, women all over the world marched in protest of his antiwomen comments, ideas, and policies. Here, women march in Paris, France.

in their own countries, many of which are ruled by governments that operate under a greater gender bias than that of the United States.

In many countries, women and girls have less access to education. In developing countries, one in four girls won't complete an elementary school education, according to the Global Citizen website. Many simply don't have access to schools or must leave school early to help with family responsibilities. War will often disrupt or end education for many students, both male and female, in countries where the government is unstable or under attack.

Globally, women are also fighting for access to birth control and maternity care. Around 225 million women around the globe don't have access to birth control, resulting in 74 million unplanned pregnancies each year, according to Women Deliver. Additionally, according to the World Health Organization, around 800 women around the world die every day because of pregnancy-related illness or difficulties that could be prevented by access to prenatal care.

Women all over the world are also frequently the victims of violence, through sex trafficking, domestic violence, or sexual assault. They often don't have access to online networks and information where they can reach out for support.

In some places, women's basic needs of safe drinking water and sanitation are not being met. Women in these areas are often tasked with the responsibility of carrying buckets of water, and this is time-consuming and ultimately takes them away from educational and personal pursuits.

PROJECT 13
WOMEN'S RIGHTS IN OTHER COUNTRIES

Different societies around the globe have dealt with women's rights in different ways. In this project, examine one chosen country's approach to women's rights and how that affects women's daily lives there.

- Choose a country and research women's rights there.
  - What challenges do women face in this particular country and how do they compare with the challenges that American women face?

Presenting a project in front of your class can be pretty stressful, but some of the best ways to put yourself at ease are to be really prepared and to practice at home.

- o Are there any historical women's rights movements there?
- o If so, when did they start?
- o How have they continued to progress?
- o What factors led to the movement?
- o What elements, if any, have slowed or halted the women's movement there?
- Print out a blank map of your chosen country. Mark the map with its capital and borders. If there was a women's

rights movement within the country, where did it start? How did geography (for example, its proximity to other countries and cultures) influence women's rights in the country?

- Write an account of a day in the life of a fictional woman from your chosen country. Where does she live? What kinds of issues would she deal with on a daily basis? What long-term issues might she be confronting? How would these issues affect her abilities to vote and share her opinions, or to marry, have children, and have a career?

- Share your map and your account with your class. You can compile your work into an online presentation, or paste your work to poster board to share.

GLOSSARY

ABOLITION The movement that pushed for the outlawing of slavery in the United States.

ABORTION The purposeful termination of a pregnancy.

ACTIVISM The practice of taking political action against or for a controversial issue.

ALLY An individual who, while perhaps not being personally affected by a political or social issue, takes the side of someone who is or may be affected.

AMBITION The desire to accomplish a task over a long period of time and through a great deal of hard work.

ANIMOSITY A strong feeling of hostility, anger, and resentment.

ANTISUFFRAGIST An individual who was opposed to giving women the right to vote.

BALLOT A means of casting a vote, either physically or electronically.

BIRTH CONTROL A device or method that is used to prevent pregnancy.

CAUCUS An official meeting at which members of a political party share opinions on candidates and causes and select a candidate to vote for as a group.

CISGENDER A term that defines an individual whose personal identity coincides with the gender they were assigned at birth.

CONSTITUTIONAL AMENDMENT An official change to the US Constitution, which must be ratified by the majority of states in order to go into effect.

FAMILY PLANNING The practice of managing the number of children in a family through use of contraception.

MONARCHY A type of government that is ruled by a king or queen.

PACIFIST A person who refuses to engage in or show support for any forms of violence or war.

PICKET An act of protest where a group of people stands outside of an organization or business in an attempt to disrupt its activities or bring awareness to what it does.

PROTEST An action, often a gathering of like-minded individuals, with the purpose of showing public objection to an individual, policy, or cause.

QUAKER A member of the Religious Society of Friends, a group that practices pacifism and encourages a direct connection between a believer and God.

SUFFRAGE The right to cast a vote.

TEMPERANCE A belief in abstinence from alcohol.

TRANSGENDER A term that defines an individual whose personal identity differs from the gender they were assigned at birth.

WORKHOUSE A type of work prison where the poor were given room and board in exchange for hard labor.

American Civil Liberties Union (ACLU)
125 Broad Street, 18th floor
New York, NY 10004
(212) 549-25000
Website: https://www.aclu.org
Facebook: @aclu
Twitter: @ACLU
The ACLU works to defend and preserve the individual rights and liberties guaranteed by the Constitution and laws of the United States.

Association for Women's Rights in Development (AWID)
215 Spadina Avenue, Suite 150
Toronto, ON M5T 2C7
Canada
(416) 594-3773
Website: https://www.awid.org
Facebook: @AWIDWomensRights
Twitter: @AWID
AWID is an international, feminist membership organization committed to achieving gender equality, sustainable development, and women's human rights.

Canadian Women's Foundation
133 Richmond Street W, Suite 504
Toronto, ON M5H 2L3

Canada

(416) 365-1444

Website: https://www.canadianwomen.org

Facebook: @CanadianWomensFoundation

The Canadian Women's Foundation works to improve gender equality and social and economic conditions for women.

Equality Now

125 Maiden Lane

9th Floor, Suite B

New York, NY 10038

(212) 586-0906

Website: https://www.equalitynow.org

Facebook: @equalitynoworg

Twitter: @equalitynow

Equality Now is dedicated to advocating on behalf of women and girls through legal intervention and taking action against human rights abuses.

Global Fund for Women

800 Market Street, 7th floor

San Francisco, CA 94102

(415) 248-4800

Website: https://www.globalfundforwomen.org

Facebook: @GlobalFundforWomen

Twitter: @GlobalFundWomen

The Global Fund for Women is a global champion for the human rights of women and girls. The group uses its powerful network to find, fund, and amplify the courageous work of women who are building social movements and challenging the status quo.

National Organization for Women (NOW)
1100 H Street NW, Suite 300
Washington, DC 20005
(202) 628-8669
Website: https://now.org
Facebook and Twitter: @NationalNOW
The National Organization for Women is dedicated to its multi-issue and multistrategy approach to women's rights and is the largest organization of feminist grassroots activists in the United States.

Planned Parenthood Federation of America (PPFA)
123 William Street, 10th floor
New York, NY 10038
(800) 430-4907
Website: https://www.plannedparenthood.org
Facebook: @PlannedParenthood
Twitter: @PPFA
Planned Parenthood is a health care and advocacy organization that provides medical care and reproductive education to women and advocates for women's rights.

FOR FURTHER READING

Adichie, Chimamanda Ngozi. *We Should All Be Feminists*. New York, NY: Vintage, 2014.

Colman, Penny. *Elizabeth Cady Stanton and Susan B. Anthony: A Friendship That Changed the World*. New York, NY: Henry Holt, 2013.

Crenshaw, Kimberlé. *On Intersectionality: Essential Writings*. New York, NY: The New Press, 2019.

Friedan, Betty. *The Feminine Mystique*. 50th anniversary ed. New York, NY: W.W. Norton & Company, 2013.

McRae, Elizabeth Gillespie. *Mothers of Massive Resistance: White Women and the Politics of White Supremacy*. New York, NY: Oxford University Press, 2018.

Neuwirth, Jessica. *Equal Means Equal: Why the Time for an Equal Rights Amendment Is Now*. New York, NY: The New Press, 2015.

Richards, Cecile. *Make Trouble: Standing Up, Speaking Out, and Finding the Courage to Lead: My Life Story*. New York, NY: Touchstone, 2018.

Sherr, Lynn. *Failure Is Impossible: Susan B. Anthony in Her Own Words*. New York, NY: Crown, 2010.

Spruill, Marjorie J. *Divided We Stand: The Battle Over Women's Rights and Family Values That Polarized American Politics*. New York, NY: Bloomsbury USA, 2017.

Steinem, Gloria. *My Life on the Road*. New York, NY: Random House, 2015.

BIBLIOGRAPHY

Aeschylus. *Seven Against Thebes* (Greek Tragedy in New Translations). New York, NY: Oxford University Press, 1991.

American Experience. "Wilson and Women's Suffrage." PBS. Retrieved February 16, 2018. http://www.pbs.org/wgbh /americanexperience/features/wilson-womens-suffrage.

Dionne, Evette. "Women's Suffrage Leaders Left Out Black Women." *Teen Vogue*, August 18, 2017. https://www .teenvogue.com/story/womens-suffrage-leaders-left-out -black-women.

Eig, Jonathan. *The Birth of the Pill: How Four Crusaders Reinvented Sex and Launched a Revolution*. New York, NY: W. W. Norton, 2014.

Exstrum, Olivia. "#MeToo Has Revived the Equal Rights Amendment." *Mother Jones*, March 5, 2018. https://www .motherjones.com/politics/2018/03/metoo-has-revived-the -equal-rights-amendment.

Glick, Hans. "9 Key Issues Affecting Girls and Women Around the World." Global Citizen, June 4, 2015. https://www .globalcitizen.org/en/content/9-key-issues-affecting -girls-and-women-around-the.

History.com. "Elizabeth Cady Stanton." Retrieved February 10, 2018. http://www.history.com/topics/womens-history /elizabeth-cady-stanton.

History.com. "Lucretia Mott." Retrieved February 10, 2018. http:// www.history.com/topics/womens-history/lucretia-mott.

History.com. "Susan B. Anthony." Retrieved February 10, 2018.
http://www.history.com/topics/womens-history
/susan-b-anthony.

June-Friesen, Katy. "Old Friends Elizabeth Cady Stanton and
Susan B. Anthony Made HIstory Together." *Humanities*, July/
August 2014. https://www.neh.gov/humanities/2014
/julyaugust/feature/old-friends-elizabeth-cady-stanton
-and-susan-b-anthony-made-histo.

McMillen, Sally. *Seneca Falls and the Origins of the Women's
Rights Movement* (Pivotal Moments in American History).
New York, NY: Oxford University Press, 2009.

Michals, Debra, ed. "Lucy Stone." National Women's History
Museum. Retrieved February 10, 2018. https://www.nwhm
.org/education-resources/biographies/lucy-stone.

Michals, Debra, ed. "Sojourner Truth." National Women's History
Museum. Retrieved February 10, 2018. https://www
.womenshistory.org/education-resources/biographies
/sojourner-truth.

National Susan B. Anthony Museum & House. "Biography of
Susan B. Anthony." Retrieved February 15, 2018. http://
susanbanthonyhouse.org/her-story/biography.php.

Office of Assemblyman Steven Cymbrowitz. "Women's Suffrage
in New York State: How New York Pioneer Feminists Fought
for Women's Rights." Retrieved February 8, 2018. http://
nyassembly.gov/member_files/045/20120210.

Stanton, Elizabeth Cady. "Declaration of Sentiments and
Resolutions." The Elizabeth Cady Stanton & Susan B. Anthony
Papers Project. Retrieved February 10, 2018. http://ecssba
.rutgers.edu/docs/seneca.html.

INDEX

ABOUT THE AUTHOR

Bethany Bryan is the author of several books for Rosen Publishing, as well as an editor and copy editor for companies like Scholastic, Skyhorse, and :01. Her previous works include *The Bay of Pigs and the Cuban Missile Crisis* (The Cold War Chronicles) and *Melania Trump: Model and First Lady* (Leading Women). She enjoys studying American history, video games, cooking, and collecting show tunes on vinyl. She lives in Kansas City, Missouri.

PHOTO CREDITS

Design and Layout: Nicole Russo-Duca; Editor and Photo Researcher: Elizabeth Schmermund